AUSTRALIAN LITERATURE

1900-1950

AUSTRALIAN LITERATURE
1900-1950

H. M. GREEN

MELBOURNE UNIVERSITY PRESS

First published 1951
Reprinted, with minor corrections, 1963
Printed and published in Australia by
Melbourne University Press, Parkville N.2, Victoria
Registered in Australia for transmission by post as a book

The original text has been reprinted except for a very few minor corrections. In the Bibliography some dates have been added or revised. References to the second edition of the *Australian Encyclopaedia* and to Macartney's revision of Miller's *Australian Literature* have been added.

London and New York: Cambridge University Press

Contents

Author's Note

To give an account of what is by far the greatest and most important part of Australian literature in a booklet of this size is difficult. The difficulty increases when the term 'literature' is interpreted, as it is here, widely enough to include all types of literary work that have contributed to the national culture; yet otherwise an incomplete impression would be conveyed. In the sections that deal with works of 'applied' literature, the subjective element that attaches to all criticism must be comparatively large, because such works have to be judged by several standards, and these sometimes conflict. Nevertheless, an attempt has been made to provide a true perspective, whatever differences of opinion there may be about detail and instance, and a running review in which the need of compression shall not squeeze out the interest and life. The author is indebted, sometimes heavily, to several friends who have been kind enough to help and advise in sections of the 'applied' literature in which they are experts and he is not. Nevertheless all opinions expressed here are ultimately his own, and for any mistakes of fact or idea he alone is responsible. For dates and other details he is often indebted to such works of reference as *Who's Who in Australia,* Serle's *Dictionary of Australian Biography,* and Morris Miller's *Australian Literature from its Beginnings to 1935* [another edition, revised and extended to 1950, published 1956, edited by Frederick T. Macartney].

It has seemed best to make all references in the text as general as possible, leaving specific references for the most part to the bibliography. Nevertheless the bibliography aims at simplicity rather than completeness. The reader is warned that both text and bibliography mention only works considered representative or otherwise important for the purposes of this review, and that many of them are out of print, though they should all be obtainable at the larger libraries.

1

Introductory

Almost all that is distinctive and by far the most that really matters in Australian literature belong to the half-century that is now ending; broadly speaking, that is, for it was with the later nineties that the period actually began. Before that there had been a few forerunners, but they had been isolated, in a society in which a national literature would have been impossible because national characteristics, national unity, and a national consciousness had not yet been attained. But a foundation was now laid, and upon it arose a literature that from the beginning may fairly be called Australian. It is split horizontally by a line of demarcation between the products of peace and national development and of wars and fears of wars; and it is split perpendicularly by the difference between 'applied' literature, whose principal object is the conveying of facts and ideas, and 'pure' literature, whose object is largely aesthetic, and in which a much greater part is played by the personality of the writer. But many works lie across the boundaries of these literatures, and the divisions between them are not fundamental.

Various causes combined in a young and vigorous community to promote at the turn of the century a consciousness of democratic nationhood. This was the matrix, but the literature that came out of it was stimulated by the renascence, as distinguished from the decadence, of the English 'Nineties', and organized and guided by the Sydney *Bulletin,* on which J. F. Archibald and his sub-editors, and A. G. Stephens, editor of the *Bulletin's* 'Red Page', corresponded to some extent with Henley and his 'young men'. This literature was, as might have been expected in the circumstances, vital, individual, simple and sometimes rather crude, and its insistence upon nationality gave even some of its best work a rather provincial air. It was a remarkable product, nevertheless. In its short stories, especially Lawson's, and in its ballads, especially Paterson's, it may be said to have made a contribution to world literature. Curiously enough, however, it reached its highest point in the work of a novelist, 'Henry Handel Richardson', and a poet, Christopher Brennan, neither of whom had anything to do with the literary movement of the Australia of their day. Not long after the ending of the first World War, with the gradual realization that it had not after all been the war to end all wars, and with the depression that soon followed, a change of attitude set in, which was accentuated by the arrival of the second World War and by growing fears of a third. In the literature that arose in these conditions, self-confidence was qualified by a realization that the world had become much more difficult and dangerous, and that Australia was an inescapable part of it. Leaders in all spheres began to look beyond their own shores, and to take into account new ideas, methods and fashions. What was written became much more sophisticated, concerned more with the revelation of character and personality by means of psychological analysis than with action for its own sake and the revelation of character through action. Writers became much better craftsmen, and in particular they learned much more of the art and craft of fiction. The defeatism of T. S. Eliot has found little kinship and few echoes in this country, but, broadly speaking, an unillusioned realism has taken the place of the romanticism of the earlier generations.

2

Ballad-verse and Poetry

The national characteristics that began to ripen just before the turn of the century were most marked in the ballad, and after that in the short story. The Australian ballad was a part of the modern revival of this form under the leadership of Kipling; but it derived more immediately from Gordon, and from that poor relation of the European folk-ballad, the Old Bush Song. At its most characteristic it is as fresh and individual as a sunlit stream into which gumleaves have fallen, and carries with it an atmosphere of careless freedom and dare-devilry that is even now regarded, consciously or subconsciously, as characteristically Australian. The best and most typical of the balladists is 'Banjo' Paterson, and after him Henry Lawson, with whose verses the stream flows sometimes through deep shade. Over the hot dry country with which the ballad oftenest deals, Paterson rode but Lawson plodded, humping his swag, and the melancholy side of his temperament found more and the humorous side less expression in his ballads than in his short stories. Allied to the balladists is C. J. Dennis, who based on the recently-discovered larrikin a sentimental and extremely amusing extravaganza that was enormously popular in its day. Behind the balladists, far less read and less obviously Australian, though still affected by the nationalistic movement, came the bulk of the poets, lyrical or lyrically descriptive; and away in the background, with a few exceptions scarcely read at all, were a number of more or less reflective poets, and in particular three intellectuals, with whom we shall deal later on. Among the most popular of the early lyrists were Victor Daley, who stands in Australia for the spirit of old-world romance; and Roderic Quinn, a 'nature poet' who possessed a certain intuitive quality that enabled him to pierce a little below the surface now and then. A few years later, though it was much longer before they became recognized, appeared the two finest pure lyrists that the country has produced. Shaw Neilson, though for the greater part of his life a bush labourer, contrived somehow to write the most delicate and ethereal of lyrics. Nature did not appeal to him, but he used it to convey glimpses of unattainable beauty, which he was always seeking. Men in general did not appeal to him either, but he wrote some warm and tender ballads, mostly about children, young lovers, and aged or unhappy people. The poetry of the second of these two, Hugh McCrae, is as different from Neilson's as a violoncello from a flute. The beauty that he worships is not supernal, but a glorification of earth and flesh. Neilson's versecraft is sufficient, even amazing in the circumstances, but McCrae is the most accomplished verbal artist of his generation; an artist in several senses, for his poetry proceeds with a rich and sensuous music through scenes and actions that are bright with colour and a succession of lovely images. His vigour and appetite for life are such that he is able to renew with fresh vitality conventional forms and types and institutions. Of the innumerable lyrically descriptive poets, there is room here to mention only J. Le Gay Brereton, a kindly and human nature-mystic, with a natural but extremely individual style. Among the lyrists of the second half of the century a woman, Judith Wright, is supreme. She is also, except for the much older Mary Gilmore, easily supreme among Australian women poets, and, along with the leading intellectuals, she represents in her different way the height of Australia's contribution to the poetry of today. Judith Wright is, in the main, a poet of love, but from a woman's point of view; from the point of view at any rate of simple, normal and adult woman, to whom the centre is not, as with almost all romantic and most other poets, the act of love, so much as what is to come of it: not the lover, but the child.

Everything she writes is charged with thought, yet she is essentially a lyrist, because life and thought sing through her veins in music. For 'Bullocky', 'The Company of Lovers', 'Woman to Man', and 'The Unborn', Australian comparisons are insufficient.

After Judith Wright comes a gap. Kenneth Mackenzie and T. Inglis Moore deal also in the main with love: the one sophisticated, sensuous, unimpassioned; the other fresher, comparatively simple beneath a façade of sophistication. And there is Ronald McCuaig, in one aspect a witty and whimsical virtuoso in the manner of some of the seventeenth-century love-lyrists; in another an ironic observer, a little in Eliot's manner, of the life of city clerks and typists. More noteworthy is Douglas Stewart, an example of the crossing of the literatures of Australia and New Zealand: his poems possess a gay, exuberant freshness, a humour that is dashed with irony, and a whimsical fancy that is often delightful though merely flippant sometimes. Peter Hopegood, who ranges in prose and verse over philology and comparative ethnology, is incidentally a maker of songs and ballads based on those of the folk, the best of which recreate in his own manner something of the magic, the haunting mystery, the cryptic wisdom with which his researches are often concerned. And Harold Stewart is perhaps the most talented and certainly the most painstaking and elaborate verbal artist among the Australian poets of today. The luminous atmosphere of his subtle and delicate poems has something about it of the feeling of Chinese painting upon silk.

Of the poetry that arose out of the first World War, that of Leon Gellert has not been equalled in this country. The second World War has not yielded its full poetic harvest yet, but one poem of Slessor's, based on a memory of El Alamein, compares with all but Gellert's very best.

Curiously enough, in a literature that as a whole is not remarkable for intellectual content or background, most of the outstanding poets have been intellectuals. Of these the first to become prominent was Bernard O'Dowd. In his earlier work he was hamstrung by the conviction that poetry ought to be a mere handmaid to social teaching: his verses plodded slowly forward with metronomic beat, laden with a swag of science and sociology, through what would have been a dry waste but for the poet's impressive personality and fiery conviction, the occasional gleam of some gnomic epigram, and a few short poems that would seem to have been written almost in spite of himself. At last, however, in two long poems, O'Dowd's enthusiasm burned through his theories, leaving him free for a glowing rhapsody about the bush, in which he saw reflected his country and its glorious future; and an even more glowing rhapsody addressed to the goddess of love and life. The first brought O'Dowd a wide circle of readers; the second, lacking local colour and patriotic appeal, has been unjustifiably neglected. Another of the intellectuals was William Baylebridge, whose considerable poetic talent was handicapped by artificialities and an inveterate propensity for borrowing both ideas and methods of expression, which he nevertheless contrived to make very largely his own. His highest achievements are a sequence of love-sonnets, whose style is markedly Elizabethan, but which contain passages of considerable beauty, and a set of metaphysical and moral poems on the origin and destiny of man. In each case Baylebridge rises at times above his limitations and becomes dignified, lofty and sonorous, the creator of an individual beauty. The third of the intellectuals, Christopher Brennan, is now beginning to be recognized as the first of Australian poets. A man of deeper thought and greater poetic power than either of the others, he lacks O'Dowd's fiery sociological and patriotic enthusiasm, and his poems are on the face of them a gloomy and self-centred monologue. But the protagonist in his best work is not the poet merely but everyman, and the overwhelming personality, the indomitable courage with which misfortune is confronted, and the rhythm and language that convey them are such that, especially in Brennan's longest and finest poem, 'The Wanderer', the reader, becoming identified for the time with a so much larger and deeper personality, is, in the Aristotelian manner, purged of his own misfortunes and his own mediocrity. Mary Gilmore shares some of the characteristics of the intellectuals and possesses also a marked lyrical gift. She combines warm humanity and a natural and un-selfconscious simplicity with a wisdom that finds expression here and there in utterances as gnomic as O'Dowd's, though of a quite different kind; some of her work is in the front rank of Australian poetry. Frank Wilmot and Frederick Macartney link not only the intellectuals and the lyrists, but also the poetry of the two halves of the century. Wilmot's disposition was based uneasily upon an impulse towards natural lyrism, which produced some beautiful poems of the bush, and a tormented vision of man's self-made unhappiness, which reached its climax in several terrible poems of war. But he had also a strong and critical sense of humour, and in later life he wrote a series of satires by which perhaps he is most likely to be remembered. Macartney is a lighter weight than Wilmot, but his poetry is more modern in tone, and it has a wit and artistry and at its best a charm that Wilmot's does not possess.

Brennan, though his thought was often subtle and complicated, can scarcely be called a sophisticated poet; there is a comparatively youthful air about the enthusiasms of Wilmot and O'Dowd; and Baylebridge is almost naïve in his efforts to find fitting expression for ideas that he felt confident were profound. But the work of at least the leading Australian poets of today belongs obviously to a later, a more adult, a comparatively wordly-wise civilization. Yet it is only, setting aside a few minor poets, in Kenneth Slessor that the influence of the leader of the moderns in poetry has been marked, and Slessor has finally worked free into a style and attitude that are modern and at the same time strikingly individual. With him the comparative lack of illusion that distinguishes the Australian poets of today from their predecessors has become disillusion. But he differs from the Elioteans in the vital energy with which he gives vent to the bitterness of his conception of life. He reached his full powers in 'Five Bells', an elegy on a friend of his early youth who was drowned at sea: a savage outburst, directed against not merely the death of an old friend and his last agony, but death itself. Equally savage in his disillusion, but without any relationship to Eliot, is Alec Hope, who has not yet collected his poems in book-form. To Hope, man is a vulgar and absurd little exhibitionist, who seeks release from a trivial and monotonous world in radio burble and comic adventure strip. His main preoccupation is with sexual love, and he sees life from somewhat of a Swiftian point of view. In 'The Damnation of Byron', he marches forward with a slow and solemn dignity through a world of gloom and horror upon waves of rhythm that are filled with individuality and power.

The third of today's intellectual poets, James McAuley, though younger than any of the others, is extremely mature; in his restraint, order, control, he may be regarded as a classic, one of the very few that Australia has produced. The outstanding characteristic of his poetry is a brooding and highly individual music, and its leading idea is that of rhythmic change through the ages, brought about by the creative imagination. But the most important of the intellectual poets of today is undoubtedly R. D. FitzGerald; except Brennan, he is indeed the most important poet that Australia has yet produced. His work blows like a fresh wind across this jaded and disillusioned world. Idealistic without sentimentality, he finds in man a heroic quality that it is nowadays the fashion—at least among the intellectuals—to ignore. Metaphysically, he surveys life as a unity, as the past continues through the present; or still looking backward, he sketches historical characters in an atmosphere of adventurous action that brightens all his work. Of the other intellectuals, Leonard Mann is a humanist and a reformer. His experience of war and depression has given a sombre colouring to his verses, but he retains a hope and an enthusiasm that are as indomitable as FitzGerald's. Rosemary Dobson, a poet of quiet humour and individual fantasy, seems to be emerging from an abstract into a more human world. William Hart-Smith, another example of the crossing of the literatures of Australia and New Zealand, in an imaginative and sometimes fascinating sequence of poems upon Christopher Columbus, reflects the impulse towards seaborne adventure that was begun in this country by Slessor and given fresh impetus and direction by FitzGerald. This impulse has been felt by Rosemary Dobson, by Douglas Stewart, and by several of the younger poets. Those who have felt it do not, however, form a school; indeed Australian writers, of prose or verse, do not tend to flock together. The only schools in Australian poetry, after the Balladists, have been the Jindyworobaks and the Angry Penguins. The first represents an extreme of Australianism. The Jindyworobaks contend that even poetic images should be purely Australian, and that Australian writers should draw upon the culture, art and song of the aborigines. The other school represents a translation into Australia of the New Apocalyptic movement in Britain; it was guilty of some absurdities, but its work was filled with a youthful and confident vigour.

Among the lesser-known poets of today, the most interesting are David Campbell, Francis Webb, and Brian Vrepont.

3

The Short Story

The short story developed along with the ballad. Its range has since widened and its methods have been modernized, but today's Australian short stories are in the mass inferior to their predecessors, and the best of Lawson's are still the best. Like the ballad, the short story of the beginning of the century was the creation of the *Bulletin,* which still has a good deal of power over it. The *Bulletin* preferred stories of a particular kind; for example, they had to be realistic, short, concise; but within the limits laid down contributors were allowed free play, and the more pronounced talents developed along lines of their own. Lawson showed what could be done both within and to some extent without the *Bulletin's* limitations. His stories are far superior to his verses. They are written simply and easily, with much more art than appears on the surface, and with a sympathetic understanding of every type of simple character that came within his experience; no writer of Australian fiction has created so many realistic out-back types. The tone of his prose is far brighter than that of his verse; it is sometimes sad and sometimes tragic, but in a dry ironic humour that is usually but not invariably quiet, no Australian writer has surpassed Lawson. His stories have about them something of the easy humorous humanism of the camp-fire yarn, but it is translated into terms of art, and a few of the best of them deserve a place in any fairly large world-anthology. Henry Handel Richardson's short stories belong to this period, but they are outliers, connected only very slightly with their time and place. They represent a mere 'shaving from a great artist's workshop'. The only published collection consists, setting aside the titlepiece, which is a kind of postscript to *Richard Mahony,* of a series of sketches of girlhood, all of which are graceful and some lovely, and several stories set in Germany or Alsace, which have something of the tragic power of the two principal novels. Richardson has had no successors and no influence: Lawson has had both, but few of his immediate successors attempted, like him, direct transcripts from life, regarding it as a rule through humorous or tragic glasses. 'Steele Rudd' deals with the poorest and most primitive type of 'cocky' farmer and his family. A little of his early work is tragic, but it is the humorous side of this sort of life that is emphasized in the main. Steele Rudd's is a crude insensitive humour, based on action and incident, which tends to degenerate into broad farce; but at least his principal characters are within their limits lifelike, indeed memorable, and his sketches are individual, and firmly drawn and vigorous in the extreme. Barbara Baynton emphasized on the contrary the tragic aspect of outback life, dwelling upon the ugly and cruel and so isolating it from all alleviation as to produce an effect of nightmare. 'Price Warung' told of the horrors of the convict system, not romantically, as Clarke had done, but with a hard and gloomy realism, in a style that may be called journalistically documentary, though it is vivid and not without a touch of rather melodramatic imagination. The Pacific tales of Louis Becke, romantic in theme and setting, are in tone and handling matter-of-fact. Becke was remarkably fertile in action and incident; he knew as well as anyone how to tell a story and could handle a tragic climax with considerable power; but his men and women are simple types that recur and recur, and they are sketched always from without.

Among the short stories of today the 'Australian' influence is still powerful, especially among those which appear in the *Bulletin,* but the power has ebbed a little; most writers of fiction turn naturally to the novel, and, if they use the other form, use it only as a side-line. Nevertheless, some of the most memorable of today's short stories are the work of established novelists and share the fundamental qualities of their novels. This is exemplified in the stories of Katharine Prichard, but there is little in them which can match the comparable parts of the best of her other work. They are set in the countryside, among types that are different from Lawson's; she shares his democratic sympathies but has little humour and prefers sharply-marked tragedy. Vance Palmer on the other hand is better in his short stories than in all but a very few of his novels; compression suits his talent, which is inclined to spend itself in analysis at the expense of action. Frank Davison is as good a craftsman as any and perhaps nearer to Lawson than most; his individuality is marked but his scope is not great. For the rest, Cecil Mann, leisurely allusive, quietly humorous, has a certain dreamlike quality and deals mostly with evocations from the past. 'Brian James' is in the line of succession from Steele Rudd as well as Lawson, but he is quieter than Rudd, less extravagant, and also less individual. Alan Marshall reaches a higher level now and then; he has something of a romantic touch: these two stick mainly to the countryside. Gavin Casey and Don Edwards deal in harder, drier styles with the town mainly, and mine or factory. As talented as any is Dal Stivens, but he tends to treat his men and women as though they were bodies on the dissecting table. The only writer of war stories who need be mentioned here is Harley Matthews, who has revealed to the life the average 'hard doer' in the ranks of the first A.I.F.

4

The Novel

The highest achievements of Australian literature are, as has been seen, by no means invariably the most 'Australian' in tone. This fact is less evident in prose than in poetry, as distinct from ballad-verse, but even in prose there is the obvious example of Henry Handel Richardson. The novels of the early part of the half-century were, generally speaking, wordy, discursive, and lacking in structure, but these qualities are very far from being characteristic of her work. She left Australia as a girl of seventeen, but her first novel was conceived and partly written before she settled in England, and all the others except the last, which does not concern us, were based on Australian experience, supplemented in one case by visits to Australia and historical documents consulted here. Richardson was not interested in local colour as such, though she advised young Australians to write of their own country, but in creating characters who belong to the life of the world rather than of any particular part of it. *Maurice Guest* is a chapter of youthful passion and disillusion, recorded by a person of imaginative vision who is yet relentless in the pursuit of the exact truth. *The Getting of Wisdom* has been called the best of all contemporary school stories, and this is if anything an understatement, partly because here also, as indeed in all Richardson's work, nothing is allowed to divert the author from the truth as she sees it, or as her principal character sees it. But *The Fortunes of Richard Mahony* represents the highest peak of Richardson's achievement, and of the achievement of the Australian novel. It is the tragedy of a conflict between the central character and his circumstances, or, in the last resort, himself; it is in the great tragic tradition, and upholds it. This is one of the world's great novels, and if one hesitates to call its author a great novelist, that is because of the comparatively small bulk of her work and its comparatively narrow range. Joseph Furphy belongs to Australia as Richardson belongs to the world; he is indeed, as he remarked of his masterpiece, 'offensively Australian'. But he is a man of one book; even apart from the fact that the subsidiary novels, or the gist of them, were part originally of the great mass from which *Such is Life* was quarried, they are comparatively insignificant. Furphy is far more representative than Richardson. Like Lawson, he reflects the Australianism of his day, but the emphasis is quite different; whereas with Lawson it is its mateship, with Furphy it is its assertion of rights. Furphy's work possesses an intellectual content and background that Lawson's lacks, and it flows with a stronger current of life. But it is narrow and parochial, as Lawson's is not; and though in his quite different way Furphy is for good and evil a stylist, he is diffuse and digressive and never such a master of style as Lawson at his best. *Such is Life* remains however the most original and vigorous novel that has come out of this country. Two other novelists whose work, though published later, belongs to the same day, reflect, though in a manner that is quite different from Furphy's, the Australian countryside. Both are extremely feministic; the second is a woman and the first appears to be a woman, or women, though her identity remains concealed. The Australian novels of 'Brent of Bin Bin' constitute a rambling and discursive saga that opens with the taking-up of the first runs in south-eastern New South Wales and extends beyond the first World War. They are not a work of art but an unorganized extract from life, and the style in which they are written is sometimes clumsy and in its affected polysyllabics even excruciating; but the conversations at least are real and the men and women are typical and very much alive. Miles Franklin deals in a somewhat similar manner with the same types in the same settings, and it has been suggested that she had something to do with the writing of the Bin Bin books; but her work cannot compare with the best of these, except in the principal character of her principal novel, who is one of the most living and original in Australian fiction. Another woman writer is Mrs Aeneas Gunn, best known for a piece of autobiography treated in the manner of fiction, which gives a visitor's impression of station life and characters in part of the Northern Territory. They are sketched with realism, humour and a romantic sympathy that becomes at times very sentimental; but the book is so alive and interesting that it has deserved the wide reading that some of the others deserve and have not obtained. With Louis Stone we turn from the country to the city. *Jonah* is the classic of the larrikin, as the Bin Bin books are classics of station life. It consists of two quite different kinds of story welded together incongruously; but the larrikin part, and in particular Chook and his Pinkey, are delightfully though romantically real; and Mrs Yabsley, the enormous illiterate washerwoman who saw everything that happened in her neighbourhood and commented upon it with ironic wisdom, is almost beyond praise. Stone's only other novel shares the faults and some of the merits of *Jonah*. The novels of W. G. Hay are all historical, and almost entirely based, like Clarke's masterpiece, upon the cruelties and sufferings of 'The System'. But Hay deals with mental rather than physical sufferings, and his principal novel is a tragedy of nervous strain, written in a highly artificial and allusive style, full of mannerisms and reminiscent of Meredith, occasionally obscure but with considerable power.

In the novel of today the current of Australianism still runs strong, though more and more writers are being attracted to the comparatively cosmopolitan cities. Freud and Joyce and the neo-barbaric school in America have had comparatively little effect upon our leading writers, but they have felt the influence of the saga novel and the tendency to run to an immense length; this indeed had already shown itself in Furphy, Bin Bin and Franklin. It will be convenient to group roughly today's novelists according as they stand out by reason of their artistry or of their vitality and force. But these two groups naturally overlap, particularly in the work of the chief Australian novelist today, Katharine Prichard; she is on the whole surpassed only by Henry Handel Richardson, and, in another way and with qualifications that are not unimportant, by the author of *Such is Life*. She is deliberately 'Australian', but she is neither narrow nor provincial, and in her width of democratic sympathy she traces back to Lawson rather than Furphy. She is much more of an artist than Furphy, and understands how to construct a novel, but though vigorous enough, she has neither Furphy's humour nor his vital and compelling personality. Her *Working Bullocks,* a story of timbergetters in the Western Australian forests, is as near to the soil as *Such is Life;* and *Coonardoo* is another Australian classic: a story of the long hard struggle with heat and dust and loneliness on a far outback station, through which runs an idyll that ends in bitter tragedy. Kylie Tennant, almost a generation younger than Katharine Prichard, has much in common with her; but instead of being predominantly serious, she has an all-pervading sense of humour, and writes of the city as well as the countryside. She carries even farther her sympathy with the less fortunate, dealing typically not with the worker but with those who are out of work, on the bare fringes of society. Her novels are extremely vital, but neglectful of construction. To the same group, in its self-consciousness nearer to Furphy and to some early work by Miles Franklin, but without Furphy's aggressive Australianism or representative capacity, belongs the single novel of Eve Langley, a picaresque and self-centred, sometimes sentimental record of the experiences of two adventurous sisters on the Victorian countryside; it is rich in incident and character and abundant in life. Allied with the group in virtue of a vigour and an Australianism that are however quite different in quality and not traceable along any literary lines is the work of four other writers. Leonard Mann is the author of the best novel that has hitherto arisen out of either World War, and of another that shows the effects of the depression in the cities as Kylie Tennant shows them in the countryside, but hard and grim and unlightened by humour. His most memorable novel is, however, a low-toned but striking picture of a small farming township on half-barren land in which elemental passions grow out of the bitter and envious struggle for a bare livelihood. The novels of Norman Lindsay, which belong almost wholly to the latter part of the half-century, are filled with a robust and restless energy and a humour that is often crude and boisterous but always realistic. Lindsay is at his most characteristic in dealing with a set of small boys who are stripped to the pelt of all manner of inhibition, and with the same types in their adolescence. The other two are to a greater or a lesser extent novelists of purpose, though there is an element of iconoclastic purpose in Lindsay as well. In a huge two-volume saga, Brian Penton debunks the romance of pioneering, telling a fierce and brutal and sometimes morbid story of the founding of a station in outback Queensland in its convict days. And Xavier Herbert deals in his one novel with cruel and brutal race prejudice in the Northern Territory. His is almost as powerful as Penton's work, and animated by a deep and sensitive sympathy that Penton's work does not possess; in their emphasis upon cruelty and horror these two novelists confer upon the parts of the world they deal with the appearance of districts of Hell.

Of those who stand out primarily by reason of their artistry the leader is Vance Palmer, who combines psychological analysis with a deliberate Australianism. He is neither so fresh nor so vigorous as the members of the other group, but covers a wide range, not so much of character as of setting, is professional in his thoroughness, and affords a valuable example to younger writers. Frank Davison seems to have gained something from Palmer and Eldershaw. His principal novels are a story of the hunting down of wild cattle in Queensland, which is in effect a kind of prose epic of the struggle for freedom; and a horse-lover's idyll of the famous charge of the Light Horse into Beersheba, again a small classic in its kind. Other leaders — at a time when so many of the leading novelists, in Australia as in England, are women — are Eleanor Dark and Barnard Eldershaw. Almost all Eldershaw's novels deal with episodes in Australian history, though not with historical characters, and in all but the first the method is psychological. In the latest, the theme is man's fundamental problem, the age-long rhythmic struggle between freedom and efficiency, worked out by means of a switch back and forward in time. Eleanor Dark, after a number of carefully finished, but here and there a little sentimental, analyses of men and women and their relationships, has produced two large and elaborate studies, at once scholarly and imaginative, of episodes and characters in Australian history. The characters however seldom emerge from the carefully-finished backgrounds, so that the novels have as a whole a certain tapestry quality. Christina Stead, who now lives in the United States, gives the impression of possessing as much talent as any present-day Australian writer, but somehow it never comes to full fruition. Her most noteworthy Australian novel is a study of morbid types in Sydney that is somewhat reminiscent of Dostoevsky. At a far remove from all these, 'Martin Mills', long resident in England, but now living in Australia again, produced a delightful if overcrowded story of a well-known Victorian family, the wittiest of all Australian novels. Of the younger writers, perhaps the most interesting is Robert Close, a promising member of the tribe of Conrad.

5

Drama

Australian drama, in the sense of drama reflecting local life and intended for the stage, was founded early in the century by Louis Esson, seconded by Vance Palmer. The plays of both reflect strongly the Australianism of the day in which they began to write, but they lack something of its vigour, and the talent in each case, though individual, is small. Both, Esson especially, are at their best in one-act plays. Fifteen years ago there suddenly appeared in book form a collection of plays by an unknown writer, Sydney Tomholt. Cosmopolitan in tone, though some of the settings are Australian; bleak, passionate at times and with occasional touches of mysticism, they seemed to promise much, but Tomholt has published nothing since. The unquestioned leader among Australian playwrights is however Douglas Stewart. Both the plays that appear in *The Fire on the Snow and The Golden Lover* were written for broadcasting. The one deals with Scott's last expedition; the other is founded on a Maori legend, so that, Stewart being by birth a New Zealander, it is a question whether it can fairly be counted as Australian. The first is impressive as a hill of ice; the hard endurance and the tragedy are none the less moving for their restraint. In the other, the poet sometimes bolts with the playwright, but the reader would not have anything omitted, though much had to be omitted for broadcasting; it is warm, humorous and rich in imagery as the other is cold, stark, severe.

6

Essays, Criticism, Scholarship

With this group we cross the vague borderline between 'pure' and 'applied' literature, for essay merges in both thesis and magazine article, and scholarship may possess no purely literary quality. The essay, depending as it does upon a fairly high level of cultivated leisure, has scarcely arrived in Australia even yet. Lacking the most suitable type of magazine, those Australians who have attempted the essay form have had to rely mainly on the larger dailies, and their work has tended towards journalism as much as towards literature. This however has not spoiled the work of the only Australian essayist who can stand overseas comparisons, Walter Murdoch. Just touched on the one hand with the academicism of his professorship of English Literature, and on the other with the journalism of his vehicle of expression, his essays are easy and conversational and whimsically humorous, with a tendency to ingenious hoaxes; there is about them a hatred of the pretentious, and a shrewd commonsense that amounts to wisdom, and they have often a serious and sometimes a rather too obvious social or moral undertone.

Frank Wilmot and J. Le Gay Brereton wrote enough in this form to indicate faculties that never came to fruition, and a small collection of A. B. Paterson's represents the journalistic essay at somewhere near its humorous best. With the reminiscences of Mary Fullerton essay merges in autobiography, as with A. G. Stephens it merges in literary criticism. Australians are only beginning to become capable of self-criticism in any sphere, yet Stephens, whose work still, after a generation, represents Australian criticism at its best, was in the fullness of his powers early in the century. As editor of the 'Red Page' of the *Bulletin,* and by reason of his compelling personality and keen critical judgment, for half a generation he reigned over at any rate Australian poetry. Almost everything he wrote was individual and stimulating, and in spite of mistakes surprising in a man of his acumen, he said many good things and many true things, and his opinions on any subject must always be taken into consideration. Of his successors in the Australian field, the most notable of those who have published collections of their work is the poet and playwright and present editor of the 'Red Page', Douglas Stewart. On the academic side, concerned more with English classics than with Australian writers, Archibald Strong published, besides some capable studies, a short history of English literature which is among the best of its kind. M. W. MacCallum's work on Shakespeare's Roman plays is imbued with a precise and thoughtful scholarship and a balanced judgment, and A. J. A. Waldock was the first Australian scholar to adopt a modern attitude in the criticism of Shakespeare's plays. A characteristic element in Waldock's work is his gentle and persuasive as well as precise and logical style. The Greek studies of W. J. Woodhouse show not only commonsense and critical insight but an individual imagination, and G. G. Nicholson's reputation as a Romance philologist extended to Europe.

7

History, Biography, Description

In the narrower literary sense, G. A. Wood's *Discovery of Australia* is probably the outstanding work in this group; for besides being a scholarly survey, proceeding easily and with discrimination from the earliest times to the nineteenth century, it is written with humour and sympathetic understanding and in a style that is simple and human. Narrower in range, but original in conception and material, the first six volumes of the official history of Australia's part in the first World War, which were written by its general editor, C. E. W. Bean, stand out in a different way. This is a history of a new kind, built almost entirely upon first-hand evidence and written from the point of view of the fighting-men in action. It amounts also to a documented analysis of the characteristics of at least the more adventurous types of the young Australians of a youthful and adventurous day; these characteristics accord perfectly with their representation in ballad and prose fiction. Bean's style is simple, direct and lucid, but stripped rather bare; it is informed, however, by the greatness of his subject and by his deep but disciplined enthusiasm. This work stands high among the military histories of the modern world. Bean had already written, in *On the Wool Track,* what amounts to a pictorial essay on the real Australian as the author saw him, and the conditions that made him what he was. After Wood in importance there were several other historians of exploration and discovery, particularly Ernest Scott, whose life of Flinders not only solved a couple of historical problems, but told a human and interesting story so well that it is among the leading Australian historical biographies. R. G. Henderson's work on the discoverers of the Fiji Islands was based not merely on the study of documents but on a careful following on the tracks of those early voyagers, as recorded on their charts. Like Scott, Henderson was biographer as well as historian; his life of Sir George Grey is, along with that of the New Zealand-Australian, James Collier, among the standard lives of their subject. The historical work of the latter part of the half-century is also notable for the painstaking and individual investigation of historical periods and episodes rather than persons, though persons may be closely involved. R. C. Mills has given the first adequate account of Wakefield's theory of colonization and its effect on the colonization of Australia. Eris O'Brien has, besides his work on early Australian Catholicism, explored and critically analysed the social and industrial background of the penal settlement and the principles and application of the Convict System. S. H. Roberts has pioneered the history of Australian land settlement, and in particular has described the rise and life of the squattocracy against a background of the conditions of the age. H. V. Evatt has made a careful study of W. A. Holman as against a background of the labour movement; this, though it does not quite do Holman justice, is the best contribution so far to the history of the Australian nineties and early nineteen-hundreds. Of two biographies by a man and woman of letters, Nettie Palmer's of H. B. Higgins is the more realistic; Murdoch's of Deakin, a model so far as style is concerned, is not well documented, and carries with it an air of hero-worship. On the borderline between autobiography and descriptive writing is the work of E. J. Banfield, the first Australian representative of writers of the type of Thoreau and White of Selborne.

Descriptive writers have been numerous, wandering over Australia and the islands of the Pacific; some of the most interesting are historical as well as descriptive, and contain ethnological material, so that they might have been considered under any of several headings. Among the most notable is a volume on Papua by the late Sir Hubert Murray, its Lieutenant-Governor and Chief Judicial Officer; there have also been a number of accounts of patrol and exploration by several of Papua's administrative officers. Prominent among these are the reminiscences of C. A. W. Monckton, an attractive but difficult person who combined a contempt for hardship and danger and for almost everyone in authority with an eye for the picturesque and an extremely strong sense of humour. The South Polar expeditions of the period have been recorded by several Australians who took part in them, notably Douglas Mawson. Other writers have dealt with adventures as such, apart from any scientific or other bearing; among these, Jack McLaren has written as least one Australian classic in its kind.

8

Philosophy, Psychology, Religion

Australia's contribution to the literature of the mental and moral sciences is much more considerable than would appear from the published books. Almost all of these have been the work of occupants of University chairs, mostly Scottish by birth, and Scottish philosophy has strongly affected philosophic thinking in Australia. The first professor of philosophy in this country, Henry Laurie, had a wide local influence, and the series of analytical studies in his history of the development of Scottish philosophy are concise and impartial, and show a keen critical judgment. Better known and valued abroad was William Mitchell's analysis of the mind as a system of experience. It was called, on its publication, 'one of the most important philosophical publications of recent years', but it would have been read and known more widely if it had been clearer and less diffuse. By no means least are Bernard Muscio's lectures on industrial psychology, the forerunner of all the later work on the subject. Muscio had the clearest and most logical of minds and a marked faculty for sifting out the essentials and making his analyses illuminating. But some of the most stimulating teachers of philosophy in Australia have published their best work only in magazines, and some of the best books by occupants of Australian University chairs were written before they came to Australia. Among works dealing with religion, the most noteworthy are those of Samuel Angus; his studies in early Christianity and its background, and in particular its relations with the mystery religions, are scholarly and full of interest.

9

Politics, Economics, Law

In politics, law and economics much has been done, but little that can be mentioned here. The lucid and sometimes penetrating analysis of modern legislation by Jethro Brown shows him as thinker and humanist, and the possessor of a natural and cultivated gift for style. Equally lucid but rather diffuse is Julius Stone's elaborate and immensely learned examination of the problems of jurisprudence on the basis of an analysis of law as logic, as justice, and as a means of social control. Learning combines again with independence of view in H. V. Evatt's analysis of the 'reserve' powers of the Crown, with special reference to its representatives in the British Dominions; E. G. Shann has an interesting and popularly-written study of the effect upon Australian development of economic facts and the attempt to control them; and W. K. Hancock has reviewed from a social, economic and political point of view Australia and her characteristic aims and institutions. Brian Fitzpatrick has examined all these aspects of the national life in a series of detailed and comprehensive surveys which are outspoken and provocative rather than dispassionate. And Colin Clark has made an essentially practical study of national incomes and the economic bearings upon them, a study in which statistics are found compatible with humanity. Entirely different from anything in this group, Alfred Deakin's posthumously-published account of the struggle for federation contains a number of fascinating character-etchings, some of which are bitten in with acid.

10

Science

In science, the principal achievement has been in the sphere of ethnology, and particularly in the investigation of the customs and beliefs of the Australian aborigines. Following upon A. W. Howitt, and of the same school and method of approach, came Spencer and Gillen, who, according to Sir James Frazer, 'laid the foundation of the science of man'. Few have been able to combine like these two the scientific with the humanly appreciative vision, and their observations are described simply and naturally, with an eye for picturesque as well as scientifically significant detail. Their work has been carried on by a number of others and extended to Papua and the Pacific islands; the authority on the Australian aborigine today is A. P. Elkin. In geography, T. G. Taylor was the first to insist that estimates of the possibilities of Australian settlement based on that of the United States were fallacious; Taylor is now resident in Canada and among the leading geographers of the world.

II

Magazines and Newspapers

The Australian magazine and newspaper are also, as we know them, products of the last half-century. It is true that Australian journalism had attained a high standard and a wide influence long before, but early in the period now reviewed the newspapers had shared in the revolutionary changes brought about by the 'new journalism'. These changes of course affected the magazine also, but to a much lesser extent. On the other hand, the magazines of the early part of the half-century shared the impetus and colouring of the literary movement of the time, whereas the newspapers, essentially practical and professional, concerned much more with world affairs, were comparatively cosmopolitan. No leading Australian literary magazine of the first part of the century has lived on until today, as several newspapers have done. The only exception is the *Bulletin,* which for several reasons is here treated as a magazine. Next after it in that day came Stephens' *Bookfellow,* which an American critic declared to compare favourably with any literary magazine in the world; it faded out, however, not merely with the decline of Stephens' powers, but because it made the mistake of trying to attract at the same time the ordinary reader and the small circle of the intelligentsia. Two other magazines deserved a longer life: the *Lone Hand,* a good general magazine, a venture of Archibald's which also faded with its progenitor's decline; and the *Triad,* a literary, artistic and musical magazine which had migrated from New Zealand and faded in the same way after the death of its principal editor, who was also its principal contributor. All these were amazingly good in the circumstances, and the *Bookfellow* has not been equalled in Australia since. Nevertheless, the two principal literary magazines in Australia today, *Meanjin* and *Southerly,* considering that only one of them is able to make even a token payment to contributors, have attained a high level, and, since both have outside backing, stand a good chance of continued life. Both are on the whole addressed to the 'middlebrow'. *Southerly* tends towards the academic and towards biographical and critical revivals of Australian classics. *Meanjin,* more closely in touch with overseas literary thought, has some overseas contributors and an extraordinary circulation for an Australian literary magazine. But the *Bulletin* remains the acknowledged literary centre, because it is able to pay contributors, because of its traditional reputation, and because of its 'Red Page', whose general level is now higher than at any time since A. G. Stephens. Of the non-literary magazines several have now reached world standards: in particular, the *Australasian Journal of Psychology and Philosophy* (now the *Australasian Journal of Philosophy*); *Oceania,* which is devoted to study of the native peoples of Australia and the Pacific; and the *Economic Record,* a review of economic facts and conditions in so far as they affect Australia.

The leading newspapers of the first part of the half-century were the *Age,* the *Sydney Morning Herald,* the *Daily Telegraph* and the *Argus.* The *Sydney Morning Herald* has taken the lead today, though in the matter of circulation neither it nor any other Australian newspaper can compete with the *Sun News-Pictorial.* This and the *Daily Telegraph* have also a good deal of political influence. Practically all the big Australian newspapers may be described as conservative in outlook, though sometimes with liberal qualifications or intervals; except the *Sun News-Pictorial,* the new *Argus* and, to a lesser extent, a few of the other morning papers, and the evening papers generally, they are conservative in form also. Rather unexpectedly, the Melbourne *Herald,* which is the principal evening paper today, is in form comparatively conservative. There is no space here to discuss other newspapers or types of newspaper, except to say that the country papers have made great technical advances during the last generation or so.

12

Conclusion

There is one indisputable fact about the Australian literature of the half-century: with all its defects and limitations, it represents an extraordinary achievement for fifty years. Yet most of its best writers are quite unknown abroad. Perhaps one reason may be that they are not much more than names in their own country; in spite of the talk about 'culture' nowadays, the concerns of the Australian community in general remain predominantly material, and its literary tastes are undeveloped. Three other facts may not be without interest to readers of this booklet. In spite of the contribution of, let us say, Brennan, FitzGerald, Slessor and Judith Wright to world poetry, Henry Handel Richardson to world fiction, Paterson and others to the ballad revival, and Lawson, Furphy and Paterson to the revelation of the Australian spirit, Australian literature stands out not so much by reason of individual achievements as of the mass of talented work produced. The second fact is that, although the people of this country are now in the main a city-bred people, in literature as in life, its individuality, its strength, its ideals still derive ultimately from its countryside. And finally, in spite of the emergence of Australian literature into a comparative cosmopolitanism and modernity, its essential characteristics are still a freshness, a simplicity, an energy, a love of action that distinguish it from the literatures of older countries.

SELECT BIBLIOGRAPHY

Authors are entered under the names by which they are commonly known, but where they are commonly known by initials only, the corresponding names are given. Dates of birth and pen-names are given in brackets. Where an author is entered more than once, only the first entry is given in full. Dates ascribed to books are those of the first editions, except where some other edition is considered preferable, and where there have been a number of editions, the fact is stated and no date given.

BALLAD-VERSE AND POETRY

'Baylebridge, William' (William Blocksidge, 1883-1942)
Love Redeemed, 1934
This Vital Flesh, 1939

Brady, Edwin James (1869-1952)
The Ways of Many Waters, 1899

Brennan, Christopher John (1870-1932)
Poems, 1914

Brereton, John Le Gay (1871-1933)
Swags Up, 1928

Campbell, David (1915)
Speak With the Sun, 1949

Daley, Victor James (1858-1905)
At Dawn and Dusk, 1898

Dennis, Clarence James (1876-1938)
The Songs of a Sentimental Bloke, 1915

Dobson, Rosemary (1920)
In a Convex Mirror, 1944
The Ship of Ice, 1948

FitzGerald, Robert David (1902)
Moonlight Acre, 1938

Gellert, Leon (1892)
Songs of a Campaign, 1917

Gilmore, (Dame) Mary (Mrs W. A. Gilmore, 1865-1962)
Selected Verse, 1948

Hart-Smith, William (1911)
Christopher Columbus, 1948

Hope, Alec Derwent (1907)
(verse uncollected)

Hopegood, Peter (1891)
Circus at World's End, 1947

Lawson, Henry (1867-1922)
(many collected editions)

Macartney, Frederick (1887)
Preferences, 1941

Mackellar, John Alexander Ross (1904-1932)
Collected Poems, 1946

Mackenzie, Kenneth Seaforth (1913-1955)
The Moonlit Doorway, 1944

McAuley, James (1917)
Under Aldebaran, 1946

McCrae, Hugh (1876-1958)
Satyrs and Sunlight, 1928

McCuaig, Ronald (1908)
Quod Ronald McCuaig, 1946

Mann, Leonard (1895)
The Plumed Voice, 1938
Poems from the Mask, 1941

Moore, Tom Inglis (1901)
Adagio in Blue, 1938
Emu Parade, 1941

Neilson, Shaw (1872-1942)
Beauty Imposes, 1938
Collected Poems, 1934

O'Dowd, Bernard (1866-1953)
Poems, 1941

Paterson, Andrew Barton ('The Banjo', 1864-1941)
(many collected editions)
Ed. *Old Bush Songs* (many editions)

Quinn, Roderic (1869-1949)
Poems, 1920

Slessor, Kenneth (1901)
One Hundred Poems, 1944

Souter, Charles Henry (1864-1944)
The Lonely Rose, 1935

Stewart, Douglas (1913)
The Dosser in Springtime, 1946
Glencoe, 1947

Stewart, Harold (1916)
Phoenix Wings, 1948

'Vrepont, Brian' (Benjamin Arthur Truebridge, 1882-1955)
Beyond the Claw, 1943

Webb, Francis (1925)
A Drum for Ben Boyd, 1948

Wilmot, Frank ('Furnley Maurice', 1881-1942)
Poems, 1944

Wright, Judith (1915)
The Moving Image, 1946
Woman to Man, 1949

Anthologies
Australian Poetry, 1941 — (Hitherto an annual, henceforth a biennial, each issue under different editorship)
An Australasian Anthology, 1946 (*comp.* Percival Serle, 1871-1951)
Modern Australian Poetry, 1946 (*comp.* Henry Mackenzie Green, 1881-1962)

SHORT STORIES

Baynton, Barbara (Lady Headley, previously Mrs Thomas Baynton, 1862-1929)
Bush Studies, 1902

'Becke, Louis' (George Lewis Becke, 1855-1913)
By Reef and Palm, 1894
The Ebbing of the Tide, many editions

Casey, Gavin (1907)
It's Harder for Girls, 1942

Davison, Frank Dalby (1893)
The Woman at the Mill, 1940

Edwards, Don (1905)
High Hill at Midnight, 1944

'James, Brian' (John Lawrence Tierney, 1892)
Cookabundy Bridge, 1946

Lawson, Henry
(many collected editions)

Mann, Cecil (1896)
The River, 1945

Marshall, Alan (1902)
Tell Us About the Turkey, Jo, 1946

Matthews, Harley (1889)
Saints and Soldiers, 1918

Palmer, Vance (1885-1959)
Separate Lives, 1931

Prichard, Katharine Susannah (Mrs H. V. Throssell, 1884)
Kiss on the Lips, 1932

'Richardson, Henry Handel' (Mrs J. G. Robertson, 1870-1946)
The End of a Childhood, 1934

'Rudd, Steele' (Arthur Hoey Davis, 1868-1935)
On Our Selection, 1899

Stivens, Dal (1911)
The Tramp, 1936

'Warung, Price' (William Astley, 1854-1911)
Tales of the Early Days, 1894
Tales of the Old Regime, 1897

Anthologies
An Australian Story Book, 1928 (*comp.* Nettie Palmer, Mrs Vance Palmer, 1885)
The Bulletin Story Book, 1901 (*comp.* Alfred George Stephens, 1865-1933)
Coast to Coast, 1941 — (Hitherto an annual, henceforth a biennial, each issue under different editorship)

NOVELS

'Brent of Bin Bin'
Ten Creeks Run, 1930
Up the Country, 1928

Close, Robert (1903)
Love Me Sailor, 1945
The Dupe, 1948

Dark, Eleanor (Mrs Eric Dark, 1901)
Return to Coolami, 1936
The Timeless Land, 1941

Davison, F. D.
Man-Shy (many editions)
The Wells of Beersheba, 1933

'Eldershaw, M. Barnard' (Flora Eldershaw, 1897-1956, and Marjorie Barnard, 1897)
A House Is Built, 1929
Tomorrow and Tomorrow, 1947

Franklin, Miles (1883-1954)
All That Swagger, 1936
Old Blastus of Bandicoot, 1931

Furphy, Joseph ('Tom Collins', 1843-1912)
Such Is Life, 1903
Rigby's Romance, 1946

Gunn, Mrs Aeneas (1870-1961)
We of the Never Never (many editions)

Hay, William Gosse (1875-1945)
The Escape of the Notorious Sir William Heans, 1918

Herbert, Xavier (1901)
Capricornia, 1938

Langley, Eve (Mrs Hilary Clark, 1908)
The Pea Pickers, 1942

Lindsay, Norman (1879)
Redheap, 1930
Saturdee, 1933

Mann, Leonard
Flesh in Armour, 1932
Mountain Flat, 1939

'Mills, Martin' (Martin a'Beckett Boyd, 1893)
The Montforts, 1928

Palmer, Vance
Men Are Human, 1930
The Passage, 1930

Penton, Brian (1904-1951)
Landtakers, 1934

Prichard, K. S.
Coonardoo, 1929
Working Bullocks, 1926

'Richardson, Henry Handel'
The Fortunes of Richard Mahony (many editions)
The Getting of Wisdom (many editions)
Maurice Guest (many editions)

Stead, Christina (Mrs Bloch, 1902)
Seven Poor Men of Sydney, 1934

Stone, Louis (1871-1935)
Jonah, 1911

Tennant, Kylie (Mrs L. C. Rodd, 1912)
The Battlers, 1941
Tiburon, 1935

Anthologies
The Australian Novel, 1945 (*comp.* Colin Roderick, 1911)
20 Australian Novelists, 1947 (*comp.* Colin Roderick)

DRAMA

Esson, Louis (1879-1943)
Dead Timber and Other Plays, 1920

Palmer, Vance
The Black Horse, 1924

Stewart, Douglas
The Fire on the Snow and The Golden Lover, 1944
Ned Kelly, 1943

Tomholt, Sydney
Bleak Dawn and Other Plays, 1936

Anthologies
Best Australian One-Act Plays, 1937 (*comp.* William Moore, 1868-1937, and T. I. Moore)
Six Australian One-Act Plays, 1944

ESSAYS, CRITICISM, SCHOLARSHIP

Baker, Sidney John (1912)
The Australian Language, 1945

Brereton, John Le Gay
Knocking Round, 1930
Writings on Elizabethan Drama, 1948

Chisholm, Alan Rowland (1888)
The Art of Arthur Rimbaud, 1930

'Eldershaw, M. Barnard'
Essays in Australian Fiction, 1938

Fullerton, Mary ('E', 1868-1946)
Bark House Days, 1921

Green, Henry Mackenzie (1881-1962)
An Outline of Australian Literature, 1930

Hart, Alfred (1870-1950)
Stolne and Surreptitious Copies, 1942

MacCallum, (Sir) Mungo (1854-1942)
Shakespeare's Roman Plays and Their Background, 1910

Miller, Edmund Morris (1881)
Australian Literature from Its Beginnings to 1935, 2 vols., 1940

Mitchell, Alexander George (1911)
The Pronunciation of English in Australia, 1946

Moore, T. I.
Six Australian Poets, 1942

Murdoch, Walter (1874)
Collected Essays, 1938

Nicholson, George Gibb (1875-1948)
Recherches Philologiques Romanes, 1921
Un Nouveau Principe d'Etymologie Romane, 1936

Paterson, A. B.
Happy Despatches, 1934

Stephens, A. G. (1865-1933)
The Red Pagan, 1904
(SEE ALSO *A. G. Stephens, His Life and Work,* 1941, by Vance Palmer)

Stewart, Douglas
The Flesh and the Spirit, 1948

Strong, (Sir) Archibald (1876-1930)
Four Studies, 1932
A Short History of English Literature, 1921

Wade, Gladys Irene (1895)
Thomas Traherne, 1944

Waldock, Arthur John (1898-1950)
Hamlet: A Study in Critical Method, 1931
Paradise Lost and Its Critics, 1947

Wilmot, Frank
Romance, 1922

Woodhouse, William John (1866-1937)
The Composition of Homer's Odyssey, 1930
King Agis of Sparta, 1933
Solon the Liberator, 1938

Anthologies
Australian Essays, 1935 (*comp.* G. H. Cowling, 1881-1946, and Furnley Maurice)
Essays: Imaginative and Critical, 1933 (*comp.* George Mackaness and J. D. Holmes)

HISTORY, BIOGRAPHY, DESCRIPTION

Banfield, Edmund James (1852-1923)
Confessions of a Beachcomber, 1933

Bean, Charles Edwin Woodrow (1879)
Anzac to Amiens, 1946
The Official History of Australia in the War of 1914-1918, Vols. I-VI, 1921-1942
On the Wool Track, 1945

'Eldershaw, M. Barnard'
Phillip of Australia, 1938

Ellis, Malcolm Henry (1890)
Lachlan Macquarie, 1947

Evatt, Herbert Vere (1894)
Australian Labour Leader, 1940

Finlayson, Hedley Herbert (1895)
The Red Centre, 1935

Fitzpatrick, Kathleen Elizabeth (1905)
Sir John Franklin in Tasmania, 1949

Henderson, George Cockburn (1870-1944)
The Discoverers of the Fiji Islands, 1933

Hides, Jack Gordon (1906-1938)
Papuan Wonderland, 1936

Humphries, Walter Richard (1890)
Patrolling in Papua, 1923

Jack, Robert Logan (1845-1921)
Northmost Australia, 2 vols., 1922

Jose, Arthur Wilberforce (1863-1934)
History of Australia (many editions)

Lett, Lewis (1878)
Sir Hubert Murray of Papua, 1949

Mackaness, George (1882)
Admiral Arthur Phillip, 1937

McLaren, Jack (1887-1954)
My Crowded Solitude, 1926

Mawson, (Sir) Douglas (1882-1958)
The Home of the Blizzard, 2 vols., 1915

Mills, Richard Charles (1886-1952)
The Colonisation of Australia, 1829-1942, 1915

Monckton, Charles Arthur Whitman (1873-1936)
Some Experiences of a New Guinea Resident Magistrate, 1921

Murdoch, Walter
Alfred Deakin, 1923

Murray, (Sir) Hubert (1861-1940)
Papua of Today, 1925

O'Brien, (Monsignor) Eris (1895)
The Foundation of Australia, 1786-1800, 1937

Palmer, Nettie
Henry Bourne Higgins, 1931

Roberts, Stephen Henry (1901)
The History of Australian Land Settlement, 1924
The Squatting Age in Australia, 1935

Scott, (Sir) Ernest (1867-1939)
The Life of Captain Matthew Flinders, 1914
La Pérouse, 1912

Wood, George Arnold (1865-1928)
The Discovery of Australia, 1922

PHILOSOPHY, PSYCHOLOGY, RELIGION

Angus, Samuel (1881-1943)
The Mystery Religions and Christianity, 1925

Laurie, Henry (1838-1922)
Scottish Philosophy in Its National Development, 1902

Merrylees, William Andrew (1900)
Descartes, 1934

Mitchell, (Sir) William (1861-1962)
The Structure and Growth of the Mind, 1907

Muscio, Bernard (1887-1926)
Lectures on Industrial Psychology, 1917

POLITICS, ECONOMICS, LAW

Brown, William Jethro (1868-1930)
The Prevention and Control of Monopolies, 1914
The Underlying Principles of Modern Legislation, 1912

Clark, Colin Grant (1905)
Conditions of Economic Progress, 1949

Crisp, Leslie Finlay (1917)
The Parliamentary Government of the Commonwealth of Australia, 1949

Deakin, Alfred (1856-1919)
The Federal Story, 1944

Evatt, H. V.
The King and His Dominion Governors, 1936

Fitzpatrick, Brian (1905)
The British Empire in Australia, 1834-1939, 1941
British Imperialism and Australia, 1783-1833, 1939

Hancock, William Keith (1898)
Australia, 1930

Melbourne, Alexander Clifford Vernon (1888-1943)
Early Constitutional Development in Australia, 1934

Shann, Edward Owen Giblin (1884-1935)
Cattle Chosen, 1926
An Economic History of Australia, 1930

Stone, Julius (1907)
The Province and Function of Law, 1946

Ward, John Manning (1919)
British Policy in the South Pacific, 1948

Walker, Edward Ronald (1907)
Australia in the World Depression, 1933

SCIENCE

David, (Sir) Tannatt William Edgeworth (1858-1934)
The Geology of the Commonwealth of Australia (ed. and much supplemented by William Rowan Browne, 1884), 2 vols., 1950

Elkin, Adolphus Peter (1891)
The Australian Aborigines, 1938

Hasluck, Paul (1905)
Black Australians, 1942

Hogbin, Ian (1904)
Experiments in Civilisation, 1939

Howitt, Alfred William (1830-1908)
The Native Tribes of South-East Australia, 1904

Spencer, (Sir) Baldwin (1860-1929)
The Native Tribes of the Northern Territory, 1914

--with Francis James Gillen (1855-1912)
The Native Tribes of Central Australia, 1899

Taylor, Thomas Griffith (1880)
Australia: a Study of Warm Environments and Their Effect on British Settlement, 1940

Williams, Francis Edgar (1893-1943)
Orokaiva Society, 1930

MAGAZINES AND NEWSPAPERS

Age (Melbourne, 1854)
Argus (Melbourne, 1846-1957)
Art in Australia (Sydney, 1916-1942)
Australasian Journal of Philosophy (Sydney, 1923)
Australian Quarterly (Sydney, 1929)
Bookfellow (Sydney, 1899-1926)
Bulletin (Sydney, 1880)
Daily Telegraph (Sydney, 1879)
Economic Record (Melbourne, 1925)
Herald (Melbourne, 1840)
Lone Hand (Sydney, 1907-1921)
Meanjin (First Brisbane, now Melbourne, 1940)
Oceania (Sydney, 1930)
Southerly (Sydney, 1939)
Sun (Sydney, 1910)
Sun News-Pictorial (Melbourne, 1922)
Sydney Morning Herald (Sydney, 1831)
Triad (Sydney, 1915-1928)

WORKS OF GENERAL REFERENCE

Australia, 1947 (*ed.* Hartley Grattan, 1902)

The Australian Encyclopaedia, [2nd ed., 10 vols, 1962, *ed.-in-chief* A. H. Chisholm, 1890]

The Cambridge History of the British Empire, Vol. VII, Pt. 1, 1933, Australia

Dictionary of Australian Biography, 2 vols., 1949 (Percival Serle)

Labour and Industry in Australia, 4 vols., 1918 (Sir Timothy Augustine Coghlan, 1856-1926)

Official Year Book of the Commonwealth of Australia, 1908—

Who's Who in Australia, 1906—